Thaddeus Kosciuszko

Polish General and Patriot

Colonial Leaders

Lord Baltimore
English Politician and Colonist

Benjamin Banneker
American Mathematician and Astronomer

Sir William Berkeley
Governor of Virginia

William Bradford
Governor of Plymouth Colony

Jonathan Edwards
Colonial Religious Leader

Benjamin Franklin
American Statesman, Scientist, and Writer

Anne Hutchinson
Religious Leader

Cotton Mather
Author, Clergyman, and Scholar

Increase Mather
Clergyman and Scholar

James Oglethorpe
Humanitarian and Soldier

William Penn
Founder of Democracy

Sir Walter Raleigh
English Explorer and Author

Caesar Rodney
American Patriot

John Smith
English Explorer and Colonist

Miles Standish
Plymouth Colony Leader

Peter Stuyvesant
Dutch Military Leader

George Whitefield
Clergyman and Scholar

Roger Williams
Founder of Rhode Island

John Winthrop
Politician and Statesman

John Peter Zenger
Free Press Advocate

Revolutionary War Leaders

John Adams
Second U.S. President

Samuel Adams
Patriot

Ethan Allen
Revolutionary Hero

Benedict Arnold
Traitor to the Cause

John Burgoyne
British General

George Rogers Clark
American General

Lord Cornwallis
British General

Thomas Gage
British General

King George III
English Monarch

Nathanael Greene
Military Leader

Nathan Hale
Revolutionary Hero

Alexander Hamilton
First U.S. Secretary of the Treasury

John Hancock
President of the Continental Congress

Patrick Henry
American Statesman and Speaker

William Howe
British General

John Jay
First Chief Justice of the Supreme Court

Thomas Jefferson
Author of the Declaration of Independence

John Paul Jones
Father of the U.S. Navy

Thaddeus Kosciuszko
Polish General and Patriot

Lafayette
French Freedom Fighter

James Madison
Father of the Constitution

Francis Marion
The Swamp Fox

James Monroe
American Statesman

Thomas Paine
Political Writer

Molly Pitcher
Heroine

Paul Revere
American Patriot

Betsy Ross
American Patriot

Baron Von Steuben
American General

George Washington
First U.S. President

Anthony Wayne
American General

Famous Figures of the Civil War Era

John Brown
Abolitionist

Jefferson Davis
Confederate President

Frederick Douglass
Abolitionist and Author

Stephen A. Douglas
Champion of the Union

David Farragut
Union Admiral

Ulysses S. Grant
Military Leader and President

Stonewall Jackson
Confederate General

Joseph E. Johnston
Confederate General

Robert E. Lee
Confederate General

Abraham Lincoln
Civil War President

George Gordon Meade
Union General

George McClellan
Union General

William Henry Seward
Senator and Statesman

Philip Sheridan
Union General

William Sherman
Union General

Edwin Stanton
Secretary of War

Harriet Beecher Stowe
Author of Uncle Tom's Cabin

James Ewell Brown Stuart
Confederate General

Sojourner Truth
Abolitionist, Suffragist, and Preacher

Harriet Tubman
Leader of the Underground Railroad

Thaddeus Kosciuszko

Polish General and Patriot

Meg Greene

Arthur M. Schlesinger, jr.
Senior Consulting Editor

Chelsea House Publishers

Philadelphia

CHELSEA HOUSE PUBLISHERS
Editor-in-Chief Sally Cheney
Director of Production Kim Shinners
Production Manager Pamela Loos
Art Director Sara Davis
Production Editor Diann Grasse

Staff for *THADDEUS KOSCIUSZKO*
Editor Sally Cheney
Associate Art Director Takeshi Takahashi
Series Design Keith Trego
Cover Design 21st Century Publishing and Communications, Inc.
Picture Researcher Jane Sanders
Layout 21st Century Publishing and Communications, Inc.

The Chelsea House World Wide Web address is
http://www.chelseahouse.com

First Printing
1 3 5 7 9 8 6 4 2

Library of Congress Cataloging-in-Publication Data

Greene, Meg.
    Thaddeus Kosciuszko / Meg Greene.
       p. cm. — (Revolutionary War leaders)
    Includes bibliographical references and index.
    ISBN 0-7910-6398-4 (hc : alk. paper) — ISBN 0-7910-6399-2
    (pbk. : alk. paper)
       1. Koâciuszko, Tadeusz, 1746-1817—Juvenile literature.
    2. Military engineers—United States—Biography—Juvenile
    literature. 3. Poles—United States—Biography—Juvenile literature.
    4. United States—History—Revolution, 1775-1783—Participation,
    Polish—Juvenile literature. 5. United States—History—Revolution,
    1775-1783—Engineering and construction—Juvenile literature.
    6. Fortification—United States—History—18th century—Juvenile
    literature. [1. Koâcuiszko, Tadeusz, 1746-1817. 2. Military
    engineers. 3. United States—History—Revolution, 1775-1783—
    Biography.] I. Title. II. Series.

    E207.K8 G74 2001
    973.3'46—dc21   2001028517

Contents

This map of Prussia from 1826 shows settlements, district boundaries, roads, and features of the landscape.

The Making of a Liberator

Mereczwszczyzna [pronounced **mera** choo vish **chi** nyah] was a small town in the province of Polesie, located in northeastern Poland, when Andrezej Tadeusz Bonawentura Kosciuszko was born there on February 4, 1746. Situated near the Niemen River and north of the Pripet Marshes, the village was home to Ludwik and Tekla Kosciuszko. Tadeusz, or Thaddeus, which means given by God, was their fourth child and second son.

The Kosciuszko family was one of many impoverished Polish noble families that owned land but had little money. The family's claim to nobility dated from the 16th century, when King Zygmunt I of Poland awarded them a coat of arms and an estate. Since that time, the family had maintained its position as landholder, with a few family members also holding minor political offices.

By the time Ludwik Kosciuszko inherited the estate, the family holdings had shrunk. Through careful budgeting and frugal living, he managed to provide for his growing family. Ludwik enjoyed a reputation throughout the village as an honorable gentleman, serving as a member of the local district council and as a colonel in the Lithuanian Field Regiment. He also held the honorary title of *Miecznik*, or Swordbearer, a court official who carried the special sword that the king used on ceremonial occasions.

Thaddeus spent his early years roaming the village and the estate. He particularly liked to spend time with the peasants who worked for his father. The great affection and respect he felt for them played an important role in his later life.

With four children and a constant stream of

travelers and relatives coming to visit, the Kosciuszko household was always crowded and busy. Ludwik and Tekla were never too distracted to spend time with their children. From his parents Thaddeus learned important lessons about hard work, simplicity, and character. But they taught him much else besides. Until he was nine years old Thaddeus never went to school. His education was left entirely in the hands of his mother, whom he remembered as "a woman of character, energy, and some education." Tekla instilled in her son an enthusiasm for the history and culture of Poland. An uncle also taught Thaddeus mathematics, French, and drawing, which became one of the passions of his life.

Finally, in 1755 Thaddeus's parents decided it was time for him to attend school. They sent him to the town of Lubieszw for classes at a school operated by the Piarist Fathers, an order of Roman Catholic priests whose primary duty was teaching. At the Piarist school Thaddeus studied

French, Latin, science, history, mathematics, geometry, and drawing.

Unlike his studies at home, at which he had excelled, Thaddeus faltered in school. The Piarist Fathers even thought it might be best for him to repeat a year. Despite his academic troubles, Thaddeus's love of history continued to grow. One of his favorite childhood heroes was Timoleon the Corinthian, who had freed his people and his country from the oppressive rule of Carthage, an ancient north African kingdom. Timoleon's example made a deep impression on Thaddeus; 50 years later Timoleon could still inspire him for, as Thaddeus remarked to a friend, Timoleon "was able to restore his nation's freedom, taking nothing for himself."

In 1758, when Thaddeus was 12 years old, his father died, leaving his widow to raise their four children. Telka was more than capable of attending to the family business. Thaddeus remained at school for two more years, but in 1760 he at last returned home to help his mother. For the next five years, Thaddeus dedicated himself to running the family estate, but still found ample time to read and study.

Although the Kosciuszko family struggled after Ludwik's death, they survived and kept intact their many landholdings. Yet, they could not ignore the important political changes that were taking place in Poland. The death of the Polish king in 1763 gave rise to questions about who would take his place. The Russians, French, and Prussians were all maneuvering to place their favorite on the throne. Despite their rivalry, the rulers of all three kingdoms shared the hope that they could prevent a Polish family from acquiring power. Meanwhile, in Poland, three of the most powerful aristocratic families, the Radziwills, the Potockis, and the Czartoryskis, were also battling over who should govern.

Finally, in 1764, the Polish *Sejm,* or parliament, elected to the throne Stanislaw II, a member of the Czartoryski family. One of Stanislaw's first acts was to create a new Royal Military Academy in

King Stanislaw II (center) is shown in this political cartoon trying to hold on to his crown while Catherine II of Russia and Frederich II of Prussia try to divide Poland.

Warsaw, which opened in 1765. Stanislaw intended that the academy not only serve as a boarding school for the sons of the nobility, but also become "a school of patriotism" in which students would be groomed for future roles as the political and military elite of Poland.

Through a friend of his family, Thaddeus secured a spot in the first class of what was called the "Knight's School." He was the 79th out of the 80 students selected. In December 1765, 19 year-old Thaddeus Kosciuszko made his way to Warsaw to begin his studies.

Thaddeus soon became popular among his fellow cadets. His gentle nature, common sense, and fairness often prompted them to call on him for advice, to settle disputes, or to voice problems to the faculty. On one occasion, Thaddeus's classmates

As a cadet at the "Knight's School," Thaddeus earned a reputation as a hard-worker. He was supposedly so devoted to his studies that he persuaded the night watchman at the school to awaken him at three o'clock every morning so that he could get an early start on the day's assignments. Thaddeus designed a clever system to make the watchman's job easier. Every morning while he was on his way to light the stoves, the watchman was to pull a special cord that Thaddeus had tied to his own left hand. In this way, the watchman could awaken Thaddeus without disturbing his sleeping classmates.

even asked him to speak to the king, who continued to take a personal interest in the school and its students. King Stanislaw II was so impressed with Thaddeus that he often asked him to visit. The king later offered Thaddeus a commission in the Polish army at the rank of second lieutenant and a teaching job at the academy.

Thaddeus's experiences at the academy were far better than they had been at the Piarist school. He blossomed in his new environment, excelling in mathematics, drawing, and architecture. He became especially interested in engineering and the construction of military fortifications. Thaddeus also took classes in English, history, ethics, and philosophy. Although among the last to gain admission to the Royal Academy, Thaddeus graduated near the top of his class. Perhaps the most important lesson the school taught was one Thaddeus had already learned: loyalty to his beloved homeland. Thaddeus's sense of devotion to Poland, which he had acquired from his mother and father, would remain with him for the rest of his life.

In the midst of one of the happiest periods in his life, tragedy struck again. Thaddeus's mother died in 1768. According to tradition, Thaddeus's eldest brother, Jzef, inherited most of the family estate, while Thaddeus received only a small sum of money. For Thaddeus, his mother's death marked the beginning of his troubles. Political turmoil soon disturbed Poland, threatening its very existence. Russian troops massed along the Polish border, awaiting the order to invade, while the Prussians were also at work stirring up discontent. For their part, the Poles struggled to defend an independent Poland, free of foreign influence. Still grieving over his mother's death, Thaddeus was concerned with the political situation in the country. Little did he realize that events were about to force him to leave Poland and to keep him away for five long, bitter years.

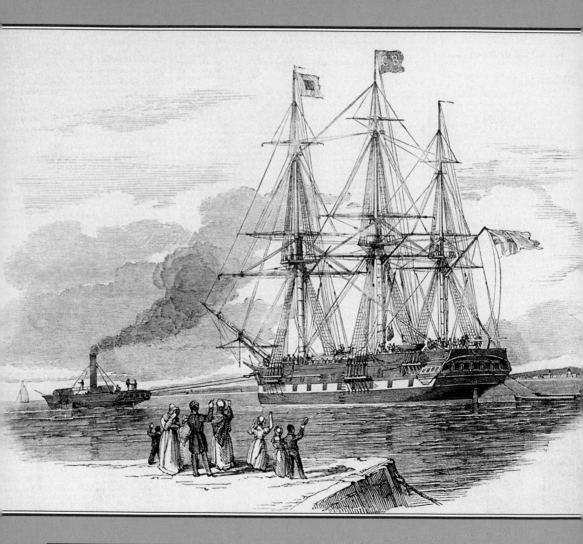

In June 1776 Thaddeus was on a ship bound for America. He was determined to use his engineering skills to help America in its fight for freedom.

"To Fight Against Ignorance, Injustice, and Inequality"

Shortly before his mother's death, Thaddeus learned that his benefactor, King Stanislaw II, planned to grant him one of four scholarships to study in Paris, France. This wonderful opportunity would allow Thaddeus to continue his training at some of the finest technical schools in Europe. Sad as he was to leave his homeland, Thaddeus was also very excited at the prospect of living and studying abroad. He accepted the king's offer, and sometime in mid-1769, Thaddeus, recently promoted to captain of artillery, set out for France accompanied by the three other beneficiaries of the king's generosity.

Upon arrival in Paris, Thaddeus immediately settled down to his studies. As a student at the famous Royal Academy of Painting and Sculpture, Thaddeus took classes in drawing and painting. Many of the sketches, paintings, and cartoons he completed during this period have survived.

Because he was not a French citizen, Thaddeus could not attend classes at the famous military schools in Paris or the nearby city of Méziéres. Instead, he enlisted the aid of private tutors and continued to study mathematics, military engineering, and artillery, all of which built on the education he received at the Knight's School in Poland. He also read French literature, philosophy, history, and economics.

While studying in Paris, Thaddeus traveled to other countries to add to his growing knowledge and experience. He visited Switzerland and Italy, where he made many friends. For Thaddeus, these journeys were part of the goal he had set for himself. He later wrote that "during the five years of my life spent in foreign countries, I . . . endeavored to master those arts which pertain to a solid government, aiming at the happiness of all."

Among the greatest influences on Thaddeus was the Enlightenment. He was especially drawn to those Enlightenment philosophers who described a new kind of government in which the interests of all men were equally represented. Thaddeus remembered the harsh treatment and difficult lives of the peasants in his homeland and believed that they deserved the same respect that other members of society, including the nobility, received.

Like the thinkers he admired, Thaddeus came to the conclusion that it was not only important to contemplate and discuss ideas, it was also necessary to act on them. "Philosophy leads to a good understanding of politics," he later wrote, but it was important to utilize philosophy in the fight "against [the] ignorance, injustice and inequality of societies and nations." Thaddeus's exposure to Enlightenment thought only strengthened his conviction that "all men are created equal."

As excited as he was about his studies and his life in Paris, Thaddeus was growing increasingly concerned about conditions in his homeland. Poland continued to suffer invasions from its stronger European neighbors. In 1772, fearful that Russia, Poland's Eastern neighbor, was growing too powerful, the Austrians and the Prussians entered into an agreement with the Russians to divide Poland. Under this agreement, Poland lost almost one third of its territory. Too weak to defend themselves, the Poles asked for help from France and England, but neither country intervened.

Thaddeus was deeply saddened by this turn of events. He was also distressed to learn that as a result of the division, his finances were in serious jeopardy, as the money he received from the king for his education had been stopped. Thanks to family friends, Thaddeus managed to continue his studies for two more years in France. Finally, in the summer of 1774, he returned home.

Thaddeus found the situation in Poland to be

much worse than he imagined. Little remained of his family estate. Thaddeus accused his brother Jzef of neglecting the inheritance, and the two quarreled bitterly. Thaddeus also learned that the division of Poland had left few opportunities for employment in military or government service. With few options available to him, Thaddeus moved into his sister's home.

In the meantime, Thaddeus returned to teaching to support himself, taking a position as an instructor in drawing and mathematics for the daughters of Jozef Sosnowski, a local nobleman who was also a powerful government official. While working for Sosnowski, Thaddeus fell in love with his youngest daughter, Ludwika. When Thaddeus asked permission to marry her, Sosnowski refused, believing Thaddeus was too poor to make a good husband. Despite her father's rejection, Ludwika agreed to run away with Thaddeus. Unfortunately, her father discovered their plans and arranged to have Thaddeus beaten up and prevented from returning to the estate. Meanwhile, he sent Ludwika away to place her out of Thaddeus's reach.

Heartbroken, almost penniless, and with no job prospects in sight, Thaddeus grew depressed. He realized that there was no future for him in his beloved Poland. He again decided to go abroad.

Borrowing a little money, Thaddeus planned to return to France, which he did in the fall of 1775. Yet, he could not settle down. For six months, Thaddeus traveled. At one point, he applied for a commission in the army of Saxony, a small German kingdom, but nothing came of it. When he returned to Paris, the public was consumed with news of the conflict taking place across the Atlantic. The 13 English colonies of North America, tired of paying taxes to England without being represented in Parliament, had decided to rebel and form their own country. Thaddeus was intrigued with what he was hearing. Here it seemed was a group of people who were trying to put into practice the very ideas of liberty and equality he had studied.

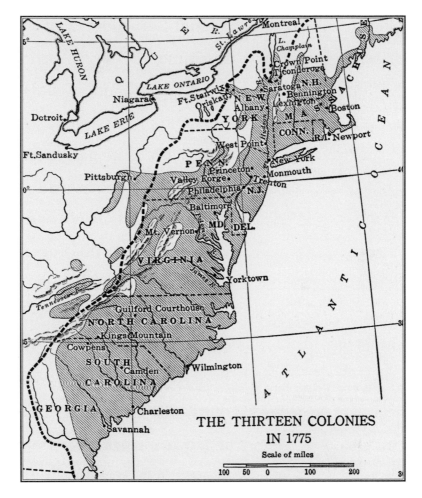

THE THIRTEEN COLONIES
IN 1775

Scale of miles

100 50 0   100   200

Remaining true to his beliefs about liberty and equality, Thaddeus was eager to help the 13 English colonies in North America gain their independence.

Not long after he returned to Paris, Thaddeus learned that King Louis XVI intended to aid the American cause. He made the acquaintance of

Thaddeus was trained in the design and construction of battering rams, towers, fortresses, and other instruments of attack and defense. In peacetime, a military engineer would build fortifications mainly for defensive purposes. In times of war, he frequently dug trenches, or tunnels, that helped troops approach and overrun enemy positions. As a result, the other soldiers referred to military engineers as "sappers" or "miners." The invention of gunpowder required military engineers to develop more technical knowledge of engineering and architecture. They now had to erect structures that could withstand not only the mass charge of enemy troops, but also continuous artillery bombardment. But military engineers were soldiers first, and, like Thaddeus, they often fought alongside their comrades.

French merchant and diplomat Pierre Augustin Caron de Beaumarchais, who had arranged for a large sum of money to be sent to the Americans for the purchase of weapons and supplies. Beaumarchais also outfitted a number of French volunteers to help the Americans in their struggle for independence. When Thaddeus heard from Beaumarchais that the Americans were in desperate need of military engineers, he offered to go to America.

By June 1776, Thaddeus was onboard a ship bound for America. Though he had no idea what lay in store for him, he knew that

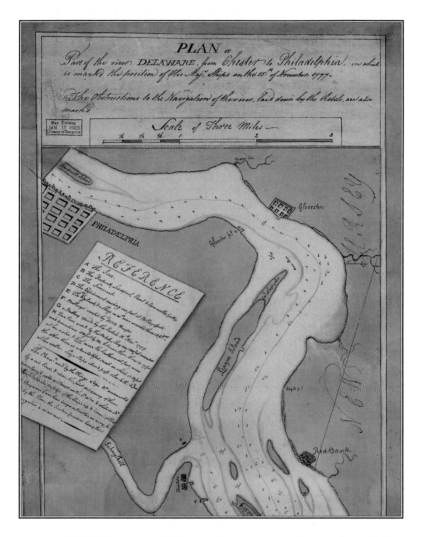

Thaddeus would have the opportunity to show his skills by building forts on river banks in America. This early map of the Delaware River shows an area from Chester to Philadelphia, in Pennsylvania.

fate had presented him with an incredible opportunity to use his skills in the service of liberty.

Armed with the tools of his trade, Thaddeus presented himself to the Continental Congress and offered his skills as a military engineer.

3

Colonel of Engineers in the Continental Army

Thaddeus Kosciuszko probably arrived in America sometime in August 1776, when his ship weighed anchor near Philadelphia. Not long after his arrival, Thaddeus presented himself to the Continental Congress, then meeting in the city, to apply for a commission in the Continental Army.

At first, the Congress was not favorably impressed with Thaddeus's credentials, nor did its members hasten to offer him a place in the army. For some time, a number of foreign visitors had come before Congress trying to secure military posts. Many were not interested in fighting for the American cause as much they were interested in gaining fame and fortune. Few had the skills of which they boasted, and most had made nuisances of themselves. As far as the Congress was concerned, Thaddeus was just another one of these incompetent men with whom they wanted nothing to do.

Thaddeus, though, was not easily discouraged. On August 30, 1776, he filed a formal application for a commission in the Continental Army. Congress did not immediately act on his request, busy as it was with the terrible beating the Continental Army had just suffered at the hands of the British. Thaddeus was becoming desperate. His money was running out, and he had no friends to turn to for help in the strange country where he had arrived.

By the fall of 1776, the Americans knew that the defenses of Philadelphia had to be strengthened. With the defeat of American forces near New York City, it was only a matter of time before the British turned southward and set their sights on Philadelphia. The Americans desperately needed a talented

Thaddeus was assigned the job of fortifying the shore of the Delaware River. The British were heading to Philadelphia and the city was unprotected.

military engineer who could construct the appropriate defenses. Unfortunately, General George Washington, the commander of the Continental Army, informed Congress that he had no one to spare. Through the intervention of a friend, Thaddeus at last secured a position working for the Pennsylvania Council of Safety. His job was to

General George Washington was a strong supporter of the plan to fortify Philadelphia. He recommended that Thaddeus design the fort.

develop plans for fortifying the Delaware River, located on the outskirts of Philadelphia.

Thaddeus set to work immediately, and quickly presented the Council of Safety with plans to build a large fortress on the island of Billingsport in the Delaware River. Officials at first complained that the proposed fort was too large for the small number of soldiers who defended the island to manage. Thaddeus agreed to scale down the design so that the fort could be of use. Finally, on October 24, 1776, the council approved "an order on Mr. Nesbit, in favor of Monsieur Thaddeus Kosciuszko for 50 pounds, as a reward for his services."

Despite the initial reaction to his drawings, it was clear to those who worked with him that Thaddeus was talented and hardworking. As a result, the Continental Congress at last offered him an appointment to the army. By the end of October, Thaddeus was a colonel of engineers in the Continental Army, receiving pay of 60 dollars a month.

Thaddeus did not have time to celebrate his good fortune. British troops under the command of Lord William Howe were at that moment moving south from New York and getting closer to Washington's battered troops. In early December, Washington and his men crossed the Delaware River in New Jersey and were soon making their way toward Philadelphia. As the Americans approached the city, Washington dispatched one of his subordinates, General Israel Putnam, to see what could be done to fortify it.

Washington was unhappy with the shortage of skilled military engineers, since those in the service had disappointed him. He knew the British were on their way, not many days behind his army, and he needed to strengthen the defenses in and around Philadelphia if he hoped to make a stand there. He had no time to lose. He was, therefore, surprised and delighted to receive word that a skilled engineer was at work near Philadelphia. Washington immediately wrote to Putnam, stressing the need to fortify the city:

> Under the Circumstances, the Security of Philadelphia should be our next object. From my own remembrance, but more from Information . . . I should think that a Communication of Lines and Redoubts might soon be formed . . . . If the measure of fortifying the City should be adopted, some skillful person should immediately view the grounds and begin to trace out

British troops commanded by Lord William Howe moved south from New York toward Philadelphia and General Washington's army.

the Lines and Works. I am informed there is a French engineer of eminence in Philadelphia at this time; if so, he will be the most proper.

A few weeks later, Washington wrote to John Hancock, president of the Continental Congress, that "none of the French Gentlemen who I have

George Washington assigned General Israel Putnam, depicted above, to the task of fortifying the area around Philadelphia against British attack.

seen with appointments . . . appear to me to know anything of the Matter. There is one in Philadelphia who I am told is clever, but him I have never seen."

Washington may have mistakenly thought Thaddeus was a Frenchman, but he also recognized

Thaddeus's talent. So did members of Congress, now so reluctant to part with Thaddeus that they hesitated to send him to General Washington. Instead, General Putnam reassigned Thaddeus to work on the construction of Fort Mercer at Red Bank, located on the New Jersey side of the Delaware River and across from the fort at Billingsport. Thaddeus completed the fort during the winter of 1776-1777.

Thaddeus's design for the defenses at Billingsport and Red Bank demonstrated his genius and creativity. Spanning the distance between the two forts were two rows of crate-like structures constructed of heavy timbers. Thaddeus had these crates loaded with stones and sunk into the water. Mounted on the tops of the crates were a number of smaller wooden beams, each fitted with a sharp iron point. These beams slanted upward to within four feet of the water's surface. Any vessel that tried to pass over them was in danger of having its bottom ripped open. Thaddeus had placed a small *redoubt*, or fort, on the New

General Horatio Gates and Thaddeus became friends when they were both stationed in Philadelphia. When Gates was transferred to New York, he received permission to take Thaddeus with him.

Jersey shore to provide additional protection.

For his work, Congress paid Thaddeus two months' salary. Fortunately, the British threat against Philadelphia had subsided for the moment, as General Howe had decided to stop his campaign before the onset of winter. Although the immediate danger was over, Thaddeus nevertheless continued to work on various projects. In February, he learned that General Putnam was leaving Philadelphia to rejoin Washington's army. Taking his place would be General Horatio Gates. Not long afterward, Thaddeus met Gates, and the two became close friends. Then, on March 25, 1777, Gates received orders to take command of the American post at Ticonderoga in New York. He recognized the talents of his new friend and knew that he would be of use to him. Gates then asked Congress for permission to take Thaddeus to New York, a request that changed Thaddeus's life in ways he could never have imagined.

Few of Thaddeus Kosciuszko's original plans for the fortification of Ticonderoga have survived. There are a number of eyewitness accounts, many of them from British sources. The British recognized that the Americans had on their side a genius military engineer. One British observer thought the defensive works that Thaddeus had constructed to be "of great strength." Another complimented his enemies, suggesting that the works were "well done and showed no lack of clever engineers among the rebels." Perhaps the greatest compliment came from a British soldier who described the fortifications as an "honor to human mind and power."

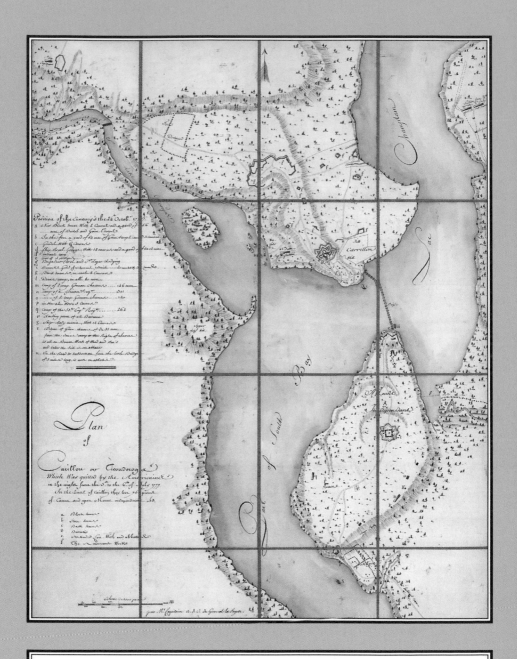

Fort Ticonderoga was originally built by the French in 1755 in New York, where Lake Champlain and Lake George meet.

Master of His Profession

For the British, the key to winning the war in North America lay in the conquest of New York. British officers in the colonies and in England believed that if the army could divide New York in half, they might eventually separate all of New England from the rest of North America. Cut off from its roots, the Revolution would wither. But in order to carry out this daring strategy, the British would have to seize Fort Ticonderoga. Washington was aware of British intentions, so he resolved to defend Ticonderoga at all costs.

Located at the point where Lakes Champlain and George meet, Fort Ticonderoga was originally built by the French in 1755. Regarded as the "Gibraltar of North America," the fort was key to the control of New York. But by 1777 it was in dire need of repair.

In May 1777, General Gates sent Thaddeus Kosciuszko to Fort Ticonderoga with orders to "examine and report the condition of that fortress; the extension (if any) to be given to Fort Independence [located near Ticonderoga], and lastly, whether Sugar Loaf Hill [located approximately one mile southwest of Ticonderoga] could be made practicable to the ascent of guns of large caliber." Gates had also written to General John Paterson, then in command at Fort Ticonderoga, to inform him of Thaddeus's coming and to tell Paterson that he was "an able Engineer, and one of the best and neatest draughtsmen I ever saw."

Upon his arrival at Fort Ticonderoga, Thaddeus met Colonel Jeduthan Baldwin, the

Ethan Allen is shown here engaged in the capture of Fort Ticonderoga in 1775.

chicf engineering officer. The two spent the next several days examining the fortress and the surrounding area as Gates had ordered. On the surface, it appeared that Baldwin and Thaddeus got along quite well and made an effective team.

But in reality, Baldwin showed little enthusiasm for Thaddeus' ideas about improving the fort's defenses, and especially for those he proposed to apply on Sugar Loaf Hill. Thaddeus believed that if a cannon were placed atop that hill, it would enable the Americans to dominate the area, making it that much harder for the British to advance against the fort.

Colonel Baldwin did not think the hill very important to the security of Fort Ticonderoga and directed his energies toward strengthening the fort itself. Although he disagreed with Baldwin, Thaddeus did not want to make trouble. He knew that as a foreign volunteer, his opinions might not count for as much as those of an American officer. But Thaddeus did write to Gates about his concerns:

> The Bridge [a floating bridge that was to connect Fort Ticonderoga with Fort Independence] is not yet finished nevertheless it must be; I say nothing of what unnecessary works have

been carried on . . . we are very fond here of making Block houses and they are all erected in the most improper places.

Colonel James Wilkinson, an officer stationed at Fort Ticonderoga, agreed with Thaddeus's proposals, and also expressed his frustrations in a letter to Gates. Realizing the seriousness of the matter, Gates wrote again to General Paterson, the commander of Fort Ticonderoga, to stress his confidence in Thaddeus's judgment and to remind Paterson that "the Enemy may give us two Months, before they come again to look at Ticonderoga; let us regard those two Months as the most precious Time we have."

In the meantime, Colonel Wilkinson decided that if Thaddeus could present his plans for the fort and its surroundings directly to Gates, he might get the necessary support to carry out his ideas. By the end of May, Thaddeus was on his way to Albany to see Gates. In his absence, Colonel Baldwin continued to work on the fort's defenses. Extremely unsatisfied with Baldwin's

Thaddeus traveled to see General Gates in Albany, New York. Thaddeus wanted to present his plans for Fort Ticonderoga and Sugar Loaf Hill.

work, Wilkinson wrote another letter to Gates describing the situation at the fort: "The works are now pushed on Baldwin's unmeaning plan. For God's sake, let Kosciuszko come back as soon as possible, with proper authority."

Thaddeus's meeting with Gates had the desired effect. Gates authorized him to carry out his plans. But before Thaddeus could return to

When General Philip Schuyler, seen here, replaced Gates, he put General St. Clair in command of Fort Ticonderoga.

Ticonderoga, General Philip Schuyler replaced Gates. Scuyler immediately ordered General Arthur St. Clair to Fort Ticonderoga to assume command. St. Clair defeated Thaddeus's plans. When informed about what Thaddeus had in mind for Sugar Loaf Hill, St. Clair rejected the recommendations. Before leaving Albany, Gates urged St. Clair to reconsider, but he refused. Instead, St. Clair directed Thaddeus to concentrate on building up the defenses around the fort and to continue work on the floating bridge.

Fort Ticonderoga was still not in good condition. The five stone bastions, which were small defensive positions that projected out from the main wall of the fort, were crumbling. Under Baldwin's direction, soldiers did not correct this situation but instead constructed useless works that offered no protection from attack. Worse, the fort was undermanned, with only 2,546 defenders in addition to 900 poorly trained and disciplined **militia** troops in reserve.

The Americans paid dearly for St. Clair's decision to reject Thaddeus's suggestions. On June 30, 1777, the American troops stationed at Fort Ticonderoga found themselves facing a substantial British force under the command of General John Burgoyne. Not only were the Americans outnumbered and outgunned, but, to make matters worse, the British did exactly what Thaddeus had advised the Americans to do. They hauled their cannon to the top of Sugar Loaf Hill, giving them command of the entire countryside. Thaddeus had been right about the strategic importance of the hill.

There was little the Americans could do. The enemy outnumbered them by more than two to one. Although the fortifications built under Thaddeus's direction were holding, it was only a matter of time before the British would break through. At 3 P.M. on July 5, St. Clair called a council of war to discuss what to do next. His subordinates quickly voted to abandon the fort. By 10 o'clock that night, the Americans silently made their escape from the British under the cover of darkness.

One eyewitness account described the retreating American troops as "badly armed, and both men and officers half naked, sickly," while the journey itself "was made with great disorder." Despite the terrible conditions, Thaddeus was quite helpful to the operation. "In the retreat of the American army, Kosciuszko was distinguished for activity and courage," James Wilkinson later wrote. "It was he who directed placing obstructions in the route, breaking down bridges," anything that would impede the pursuit of the British troops.

The loss of Fort Ticonderoga was disastrous for the American cause. Not only did they sacrifice the "Gibraltar of North America," but they had also failed to destroy supplies, including 349,760 pounds of flour, 143,830 pounds of salted meat, plus ammunition, guns, and other equipment that the British could now put to use against them. Even while he was organizing the retreat, Thaddeus feared that the loss of the fort meant the end of the American quest for independence. But he did not have time to think about the possible consequences for long. New orders from General Schuyler had arrived, and Thaddeus needed to act quickly.

British forces led by General John Burgoyne defeated the Continental Army by taking strategic positions on Sugar Loaf Hill.

With the British troops under Burgoyne thought to be moving toward Albany, the Americans now needed to stop them, or at least to slow them down. On July 16, 1777, Thaddeus, now at Fort Edward, New York, received orders to come up with a series of delaying tactics to hinder the British

To recognize Thaddeus's contributions to the American victory at Saratoga, General Horatio Gates lobbied Congress to promote Thaddeus to the rank of colonel. At that time Congress was embroiled in a controversy with French officers, some of whom had not seen action, who were appealing for promotions. Many members of Congress thought that promoting Thaddeus would cause hard feelings among the French, whom the Americans needed as allies. When Thaddeus heard of the potential complications, he wrote to Gates, asking him to drop the matter. Despite his lost promotion, Thaddeus is often referred to as "Colonel Kosciuszko" in many pieces of surviving correspondence.

advance. In a letter to Thaddeus, Schuyler outlined his plan: "I have sent one of the Quartermasters to Saratoga and the post below to bring up all the Axes which can be collected, and to deliver them to you. Col. Lewis has my orders to send you a horse immediately." In addition, Thaddeus would have at his disposal about 1,000 soldiers to aid his efforts.

Not waiting for the troops to arrive, Thaddeus immediately set out to survey the land. His first objective was to stall Burgoyne's march from the south. With the arrival of the troops, Thaddeus, using his engineering skills, set out to harass the British.

First, he and his men chopped down trees along the narrow, winding roads. Every 10 or 12 yards, the soldiers dragged the trees into the road to create obstructions. To make it more difficult for the British to remove the trees, Thaddeus ordered the solders to intertwine the branches so that the trunks could not easily be dragged aside.

While some soldiers chopped, others set about destroying the small bridges in the area, which would take the British time to repair. Still others piled fallen trees into the streams and creeks, causing the countryside to flood. Thaddeus had them roll boulders into the larger waterways, which would slow any small British ships traveling toward Albany. The Americans also burned crops and drove away livestock, so the British would have a more difficult time finding food and supplies. Nature cooperated with the Americans. Heavy rains turned the roads into seas of mud, making them hard to travel through.

Thaddeus's tactics worked brilliantly.

Burgoyne's army, which had been marching up to 18 miles a day, now barely covered 1 mile a day. Thaddeus's efforts gained the Americans almost a month in which to reorganize their shattered forces and acquire desperately needed supplies and ammunition.

In early August, Thaddeus learned that the Continental Congress had recalled General Schyuler, and that his old friend Horace Gates was again commander of the Northern army. On September 6, 1777, American forces began their offensive against Burgoyne. Gates sent Thaddeus to scout locations to anchor the American army.

He found what he thought was the perfect spot. To the north of the American post at Stillwater, Thaddeus sighted a hilly area near the western bank of the Hudson River. He reasoned that if artillery were placed along the hills, known as Bemis Heights, the Americans would command the road that ran between the river and hills. As soon as he reported his findings,

The left bank of the Hudson River in New York is shown here. The Americans and British fought for over two weeks for control of the area.

Gates deployed 1,000 men to the area to construct defensive works.

The resulting entrenchments built under Thaddeus's supervision and to his directions consisted of dirt, logs, and fence rails fronted by a barrier of felled trees with sharpened boughs. The works stretched for nearly a mile, starting at the narrow river bank and moving up the slope of the hill and across the plateau. Thaddeus also constructed a second line of fortifications just south of the hill.

The combination of Thaddeus's brilliant defenses and Gates's able leadership stopped the advancing British forces. For a little more than two weeks, the Americans and the British clashed at Saratoga, New York. Burgoyne's troops suffered massive casualties as well as the loss of food and supplies. Finally, on October 17, 1777, with his soldiers surrounded and no real chance of escape, Burgoyne surrendered.

The American victory at Saratoga was one of the most important of the Revolutionary War. The defeat forced the British to abandon Fort Ticonderoga and to retreat from other positions in New York as well. Had it not been for Thaddeus's feats of military engineering, the American effort might have failed, and quite possibly the War for Independence would have been lost. General Gates wrote letters to General Washington to praise Thaddeus.

Fort Ticonderoga had been captured by Burgoyne's forces in July 1777 as part of the British plan to advance to Albany.

General Washington, in turn, reported to Congress that he had "been well informed that the engineer in the Northern Army, Kosciuszko I think his name is, is a gentleman of science and merit. From the character I have had of him, he is deserving of notice."

British General Burgoyne surrendered to the Americans on
October 17, 1777, at Saratoga, New York.

The Key to America

"**W**est Point is as barren of news as the mountains that surround it," wrote Thaddeus to General Gates in the spring of 1779. By that time, he had been at the remote outpost for a little more than a year. Although friends sometimes visited him, Thaddeus still felt lonely on occasion. Yet, since his arrival the previous March, Thaddeus had been continually busy with his latest project: the construction of a fortress that would finally establish American control of the Hudson River.

Despite the American victory at Saratoga in 1777, there was no guarantee that the British would not try again to take New York. Particularly vulnerable were the Hudson Highlands, a series of rugged hills, deep ravines, and high cliffs located above the river, about 45 miles north of New York City. If the highlands could be secured, the Americans would have an easier time defending the area. It was later decided that the best place to build the proposed fortifications was a site known as West Point, located just north of New York City, where the Hudson River narrowed.

To undertake construction of a new fort, Congress first appointed a Frenchman, Lieutenant Colonel Louis de la Radière. Almost immediately, problems arose. Arriving at the site in January 1778, Radière found the land rocky and hard to work, the cold winter weather adding to the difficult conditions. Since he also lacked adequate shelter, tools, building materials, and manpower, Radière became increasingly unhappy with the assignment. In March 1779, he abandoned the project in disgust. To fill the void, Gates recommended Thaddeus to the Board of War.

Shown here is the Hudson River as seen from West Point. Thaddeus was assigned the task of building fortifications to protect the Hudson Highlands.

Thaddeus arrived in West Point on March 26. Despite the bad weather and the shortage of manpower, Thaddeus plunged into the project with his usual enthusiasm. He planned to erect a chain of forts and outposts on the high ground that would protect the plains below. He also ordered the construction of a water battery, a permanent barracks, and other defensive barriers to provide more protection.

One of the most ambitious of the West Point building projects was the large chain barrier that was part of the water battery. The barrier extended the entire width of the river and consisted of a series of wrought iron chains and a large number of logs, each about 18 feet in length and 15 inches in diameter. The logs were attached to the chain, as were a number of anchors that helped secure the barrier. When an enemy boat passed over the chain, it would be ensnared and at the mercy of the Americans.

When the United States sought to establish a national military academy, it was Thaddeus who suggested locating it at West Point. Although none of the fortifications that Thaddeus built at West Point has survived, the cadets have not forgotten him. On the grounds of the school is a monument in his honor bearing the inscription: "To the hero of two worlds." The cadets have also preserved the site where Thaddeus tended his garden, which today is known as "Kosciuszko's Garden."

When he was not busy with the fort, Thaddeus constructed a small shanty, where he hoped one day to receive other Poles who had come to fight against the British. He even laid out a small garden, known as "Kosciuszko's Garden," by carrying baskets of soil to a secluded spot along the cliffs overlooking the river and planting flowers and vegetables. There he spent time thinking not only about his homeland, but also about the daily problems he confronted in building the fortress. Thaddeus also shared the meager bounty from his garden with his men and their British prisoners of war.

Two events brightened Thaddeus's stay at West Point. The first was the news he received in the fall of 1779 that he had been appointed head of the Corps of Engineers for the Northern army. The second was meeting General Washington, who came to West Point to inspect the fortifications and to commend Thaddeus for his contributions to the American war effort.

By the end of July 1780, Thaddeus had completed the West Point fort. It was a magnificent effort, ahead of its time in planning and construction. Stretched across the hills were small redoubts jutting out from the main fort. Behind the main structure were six separate fortifications rising in tiers to the top of the hill. Two lookout posts guarded the eastern shore. At the highest point of the hills Thaddeus placed a number of barricades, each armed with its own cannon.

With the construction of the fort at West Point, Thaddeus had effectively denied the British access to the Hudson River Valley. The fort thus also protected the valuable farm land surrounding the river, so necessary to help the Northern army. As one contemporary noted, "[Kosciuszko] . . . gave the fortifications [at West Point] such strength that they frightened the very enemy from all temptations of even trying to take the Highlands." General Washington himself simply conveyed the

After Thaddeus completed the fort at West Point, he joined General Nathanael Green and the southern army in the Carolinas.

sentiments of a grateful nation when he wrote of Thaddeus's accomplishments: "the American people are indebted."

This monument to Thaddeus stands at West Point.

6

The Purest Son of Liberty

With the completion of the West Point fortifications in the summer of 1780, Thaddeus asked for another assignment. Writing to Washington, he begged to leave the Corps of Engineers and be given a command in the light infantry with the army of the south. Washington agreed to let Thaddeus go south, but only as an engineer.

Thaddeus was thrilled, especially when he found out that he would be reunited with his friend Horatio Gates, who had been sent to command troops in the south. On August 7, 1780, Thaddeus left West Point for Philadelphia to visit friends before traveling to his assignment.

Just as Thaddeus was preparing to join Gates, he received word that his friend had suffered a terrible defeat at the Battle of Camden in South Carolina. Gates and his men were headquartered in North Carolina, planning their next move, when Thaddeus arrived in the fall of 1780. Once there, he learned that he would not be serving under his friend, but with General Nathanael Greene, the new commander of the Southern army. Thaddeus soon became one of Greene's most trusted officers. The first order of business was getting the American army out of harm's way. The task fell to Thaddeus once more to slow the progress of the British troops while Greene escaped with his men.

To carry out Greene's plan, Thaddeus surveyed the land around the Catawba and Pedee Rivers, searching for a place where troops could safely camp and prepare to make their retreat. He selected a site near the Pedee, and in late December 1780 Greene moved his troops there. Thaddeus's next assignment was to oversee the construction of a number of flat-bottomed boats that would transport men and supplies.

Throughout the winter of 1780–1781 Thaddeus proved very valuable to Greene. Not only did he produce the needed boats, he ordered the construction of several earthworks fortifications that protected the American troops in their effort to escape. The "Race to the Dan" proved a turning point for the Americans, allowing them time to reorganize and pursue the British. Greene's tactics combined with Thaddeus's skill wore out the British and exhausted their supplies so that they had little choice but to withdraw into Virginia. Not only had the Southern army freed the Carolinas of the British menace, but they had helped to set the stage for the British entrapment and surrender at Yorktown.

During the summer of 1781, Thaddeus used his skills at the Battle of Ninety-Six in western South Carolina. Only a year before, the British had fortified the strategically important frontier town. On May 21, 1781, Thaddeus and Greene set out under cover of darkness to survey the area. At one point they passed so close to the enemy that they were fired upon. From May 22 through June 18, 1781, Greene, along with 1,000 men, staged the longest siege of the Revolutionary War. Thaddeus's job was to dig a number of trenches. These trenches were dug toward the fort, often in a zigzag pattern so that the soldiers were not exposed to gunfire from the fort.

Working around the clock, Thaddeus and his men completed the trenches, even though they drew constant fire from the enemy. On one occasion, a small detachment of British soldiers ambushed Thaddeus and his workers. They escaped, but lost their tools. To defend themselves, the Americans returned fire. Thaddeus instructed them in the use of "African Arrows," which were dipped in oil and then set ablaze. Using this primitive but effective weapon, the Americans intended to set fire to the British fortifications.

In the end, the Americans pulled back, unable to force the British from the Ninety-Six fort. Afterward, other officers, such as "Light Horse" Harry Lee, criticized Thaddeus for

Henry Lee criticized Thaddeus for moving too slowly in building trenches for the American soldiers to use in the Battle of Ninety-Six.

moving too slowly in digging the approaches. If he had moved more quickly, his critics charged, the Americans might have had a better chance of taking the fort. But Nathanael Greene defended the actions of his chief engineer.

After the siege, Greene sent Thaddeus to North

Carolina, where he helped complete a number of blockhouses and other fortifications to protect valuable supplies and provisions. It is not known when Thaddeus rejoined Greene and the army, but he was with Greene in South Carolina when news came of the British surrender on October 19, 1781 at Yorktown, Virginia.

Thaddeus's last act as chief engineer for American forces was his service in Charleston, South Carolina, where, during the summer of 1781, he received his first opportunity to lead troops into battle as the commander of a small infantry unit and two squadrons of **dragoons**. Thaddeus was in charge of coordinating scouting activities to monitor the movement of British troops in Charleston and was also instrumental in organizing the blockade that at last broke British resistance. Finally, on December 14, 1782, the chief engineer of the Southern army, Colonel Thaddeus Kosciuszko, was among the first to enter Charleston. The war was finally over for Thaddeus.

In recognition for "his long, faithful and

meritorious service," to the American cause, the Continental Congress promoted Thaddeus to the rank of brigadier general. He also received a note for back pay in the amount of $12, 280.49, to be paid in installments, and a grant of 500 acres of land in Ohio, near the present city of Columbus.

Thaddeus was also made an honorary member of the Society of the Cinncinnati, a patriotic organization of which George Washington was president. This group presented Thaddeus with a special medal, the Order of Cincinnati. The blue and white ribbon decorated with a gold eagle often appeared on portraits of Thaddeus. Washington also presented Thaddeus with the more personal gift of a sword and set of pistols, and as a gesture of his thanks, a cameo ring bearing the seal of the Society of Cinncinnati. Though Thaddeus was also eligible for American citizenship, he never pursued it. He never intended to stay in America. He was a Pole, and the time had come to return home "to be of use to his country."

Thaddeus left the United States on July 15, 1784. For the next several years, he devoted himself to the

While in the United States, Thaddeus had contact with African-American slaves, some of whom were kept by his friends and colleagues. The slaves reminded him of the peasants in his homeland. On his visit to America in 1797, Thaddeus drew up his last will and testament with his friend Thomas Jefferson as a witness. In his will, Thaddeus asked that Jefferson take the money left in Thaddeus's estate and use it to purchase the freedom of slaves, "giving them Liberty in my name." The money was also be used to help the freedmen and women to receive an education and find employment.

liberation of his beloved Poland. He returned to the United States once more in 1797. He visited Philadelphia, where he formed a lasting friendship with Thomas Jefferson. In 1815, Thaddeus, saddened by the recurring political turmoil in Poland, moved to Switzerland, where he died in 1817. In 1819, Thaddeus's remains were taken to Krakow, Poland, where he was buried among the tombs of Polish kings.

Thaddeus Kosciuszko made enormous contributions to the American Revolution. He dedicated himself to the cause of liberty and independence– a cause to which his commitment never wavered. He was modest and cordial, and more than once

Thomas Jefferson called Thaddeus a "son of liberty." Thaddeus asked Jefferson to make sure the terms of his will were properly carried out.

proved himself a loyal friend and devoted comrade. With those less fortunate or those under his command, Thaddeus shared all he had. Perhaps the greatest compliment ever paid him came from Thomas Jefferson, who wrote that Thaddeus Kosciuszko was "as pure a son of liberty as I have ever known."

GLOSSARY

battery–a group of large guns or cannons.

colleagues–acquaintances, coworkers.

commission–receiving of a military rank.

dragoons–members of a mounted military unit.

earthworks–a defensive wall made of dirt used to defend a military position.

eminence–position of great authority.

endeavor–a serious attempt.

estate–a large piece of land with a large house.

flanking–to attack or move around the right or left side of an opposing force.

fortification– a military fort.

liberator–one who works for freedom for a people or a country.

militia–a group of civilian men called into the military during emergencies.

nobility–a group of people of high birth, and who often have power, wealth, and land.

peasants–farmers or workers.

redoubt–a small, defensive structure used to guard a pass or stop the approach of an enemy force.

vast–large.

vulnerable–in danger of being harmed or injured.

CHRONOLOGY

1746	Born on February 4 in Mereczówszczyzna, Poland.
1765	Attends Knight's School.
1769–70	Leaves Poland to attend school in France.
1774	Returns home to Poland, works as a tutor.
1775	Leaves Poland to return to France.
1776	Leaves France for America to volunteer his services for the American Revolution.
1776–77	Arrives in Philadelphia, begins work on fortifications at Billingsport and Red Bank; receives commission in the Continental army as lieutenant colonel.
1777	Arrives at Fort Ticonderoga to begin work on fortifications; participates in retreat; constructs delaying tactics against British at the Battle of Saratoga.
1778–80	Assigned to the construction of West Point fortifications; is appointed chief of Engineering Corps of the Northern army.
1780	Assigned as chief engineer to Southern army under General Nathanael Greene; helps coordinate crossing of American troops over Yadkin and Dan Rivers.
1781	Participates in the Battle of Ninety-Six; assigned to command troops during siege of Charleston.
1783	Awarded rank of brigadier general; receives the Order of Cincinnati Medal.
1784	Leaves the United States to return to Poland.
1797	Returns to the United States on a visit.
1817	Dies in Solothurn, Switzerland, on October 15.

REVOLUTIONARY WAR TIME LINE ═══

1765   The Stamp Act is passed by the British. Violent protests against it break out in the colonies.

1766   Britain ends the Stamp Act.

1767   Britain passes a law that taxes glass, painter's lead, paper, and tea in the colonies.

1770   Five colonists are killed by British soldiers in the Boston Massacre.

1773   People are angry about the taxes on tea. They throw boxes of tea from ships in Boston harbor into the water. It ruins the tea. The event is called the Boston Tea Party.

1774   The British pass laws to punish Boston for the Boston Tea Party. They close Boston harbor. Leaders in the colonies meet to plan a response to these actions.

1775   The battles of Lexington and Concord begin the American Revolution.

1776   The Declaration of Independence is signed. France and Spain give money to help the Americans fight Britain. Nathan Hale is captured by the British. He is charged with being a spy and is executed.

1777   Leaders choose a flag for America. The American troops win some important battles over the British. General Washington and his troops spend a very cold, hungry winter in Valley Forge.

1778   France sends ships to help the Americans win the war. The British are forced to leave Philadelphia.

1779	French ships head back to France. The French support the Americans in other ways.
1780	Americans discover that Benedict Arnold is a traitor. He escapes to the British. Major battles take place in North and South Carolina.
1781	The British surrender at Yorktown.
1783	A peace treaty is signed in France. British troops leave New York.
1787	The U.S. Constitution is written. Delaware becomes the first state in the Union.
1789	George Washington becomes the first president. John Adams is vice president.

FURTHER READING

Davis, Burke. *Heroes of the American Revolution*. New York: Random House, 1971.

Kent, Deborah. *The American Revolution: "Give Me Liberty or Give Me Death."* New York: Enslow Publishers, 1994.

Meltzer, Milton, ed. *The American Revolutionaries: A History in Their Own Words*. New York: HarperTorch, 1993.

Moore, Kay and Daniel O'Leary. *If You Lived at the Time of the American Revolution*. New York: Scholastic Trade, 1998.

Reeder, Red. *Bold Leaders of the American Revolution*. Boston: Little, Brown, 1973.

PICTURE CREDITS

INDEX

ABOUT THE AUTHOR

MEG GREENE earned a bachelor's degree in history at Lindenwood College in St. Charles, Missouri, and master's degrees from the University of Nebraska at Omaha and the University of Vermont. Ms. Greene is the author of 10 other books, writes regularly for *Cobblestone Magazine* and other publications, and serves as a contributing editor for *Suite101.com's* "History for Children." She makes her home in Virginia.

Senior Consulting Editor **ARTHUR M. SCHLESINGER, JR.** is the leading American historian of our time. He won the Pulitzer Prize for his book *The Age of Jackson* (1945), and again for *A Thousand Days* (1965). This chronicle of the Kennedy Administration also won a National Book Award. He has written many other books, including a multi-volume series, *The Age of Roosevelt*. Professor Schlesinger is the Albert Schweitzer Professor of the Humanities at the City University of New York, and has been involved in several other Chelsea House projects, including the Colonial Leaders series of biographies on the most prominent figures of early American history.